Losing Sunshine.

Beth H.

BookLeaf
Publishing

Presentation by *BookLeaf Publishing*

Web: www.bookleafpub.com

E-mail: info@bookleafpub.com

ISBN: 9789357618502

First edition 2022

Sunshine.

And so it begins.

I love you too deeply,
I love you too much,
I love the sound of your voice
And the way that we touch.
I love how you smell
And the way that you hold me
It makes me forget all my troubles,
I'm no longer lonely.
I love when you kiss me,
You make my knees weak,
My heart rate certainly reaches its peak.
I love how you look at me,
You make me blush,
It is such an adrenaline rush.
I love how you reach for my hand,
Ever so slow,
It makes the butterfly flutterings grow.
I love the way that you smile,
And the way that you laugh,
I love all of the joy you've brought to my life.
I love you today
As I have from the start,
And I'll love you forever
With all of my heart.

I get it now.

I love you for so many reasons and none at the
same time. You make me happy. You make me
smile. You make me feel seen. It's easy to talk to
you, I can be myself with you. You don't try to
change me, you accept me for who I am. I would
rather spend the day doing nothing with you,
than be doing something with anyone else.
Because you comfort me, or try, lol. I can fall
apart and I know you will put me back together.
You're not judgmental. You listen to me. Your
smile makes my heart want to burst. I love the
way you hold me tightly when we hug. I love
you because you know when something is
wrong, you just know. You call me out on my
shit, which can be a little frustrating, but at least
it shows you care. I love you because you're
amazing. And it's more than just the physical
attraction. I love who you are as a person.
You're so sensitive and caring. Even though you
try not to be, you are. You're kind. You're
thoughtful. I love you. Meeting you was meeting
a piece of me that I didn't know was missing.
And I know that's corny, but it's true for me.
And I get it now. I never really got it before. I
love you.

And you said.

because you are unique and special. you care so much for me and love me so much. i trust you so much and you have allowed me to open up with you in ways that are extremely difficult for me to do so. you are the one person in this world who can give me so much hope and faith. i love that you pay attention to every detail that goes on in this life. big or small. you are down to earth and i adore that so much. you have a big heart for people who i would be indifferent about and i love that about you. i love that you have been through so much and still give every day your all. i love that you can be having the worst day and still find time in your heart to be there for me... you deserve so much from this world and from me. you are too pure. i love that you hold me with a grip that proves you indeed love. for the many reasons why i love you. i love you because you are you. i am so very happy that i have met you. i am so happy that i can call you ... mine. i love you so much that i wish to hold you and never let go. you are the love of my life and i mean that.

Will you?

Will you kiss me everyday?
Or is no what you will say?
Will you hold my hand to show that you are
mine?
Or will you say that that is not fine?

Will you comfort me when I am sad?
Or will my emotions make you mad?
Will you take care of me when I am sick?
Or will that make you leave the room quick?

Will you hold me every night?
Never leave in the middle of a fight?
Will you always make things right?
If I'm crying, hold me tight?

Please say you will never leave me
Please say with me you'll always want to be
Tell me that you'll love me everyday
Tell me we'll be together come what may
Promise me you will love me forever
Promise me leaving me won't cross your mind
ever

You know you are my everything.

You know are my one and only.
You stopped me from being oh, so lonely.
We plan our future as if we have a clue.
But really, I never want to lose you.
I really want to be your wife.
I want to be with you for all my life.

Mirror, mirror.

Mirror, mirror on the wall,
He's the fairest of them all,
Couldn't help but answer the call;
Inevitably then, I did fall.
Mirror, mirror leaning there,
Why lure me into his lair?
It is filled but with despair,
But leave now, I do not dare.
Mirror, mirror you're a liar!
Filled my heart up with desire,
Now the situation's dire.
A replacement heart for hire?
Mirror, mirror, let me know.
How will I ever let him go?
Before he deals that fatal blow.
Does he love me? The answer's no.

Was it worth it.

I hear your voice, in the deafening silence. Your face leers at me through the darkness, even when my eyes are closed. The winds carry your scent. You're everywhere. And yet you're nowhere. I'm haunted by your memory. I wish to drink you away, smoke you away, pop a pill and forget about you. And so I do, a futile attempt to pretend that you never existed. You're integrated into my being, I can't get rid of you, without losing myself. But I have to, and I will. Because I'd rather feel nothing, than everything I do. The pain is unbearable, I just want it to stop. Take a dagger, stab my heart, bleed you out. Fry my brain, the cells that carry every memory of you. But I'm a coward, and I can't. Was it worth it?

Once again.

Tonight, once again, I wish,
To be in your embrace,
The happiness that would bring,
To know that you are mine.
I miss you oh so much,
I cry myself to sleep each night,
My mind is plagued with doubt,
Sometimes I just wanna shout.
Why did you have to leave.
Sometimes I just can't breathe.
I hurt so much inside,
Have no one to confide,
It hasn't gotten easier.
These feelings I've suppressed,
But they have not become less,
Peace of mind, I'll never find.

Games you play.

Intense fire.
Passion.
Desire.
But is it just a game?
Are you really that lame?

Burnt out?
Fizzled?
Doubt?
If you're tired of me,
Then you need to set me free.

Bandaid rip.
Ghost.
Dip.
I don't play that game.
I'll just turn off the flame.

Lies.

You lied? I cried.
You flirt. I hurt.
You forgot? I remember.
You promised. I kept it.
You're done? I was trying.
You love me. Stop lying.

Refresh.

I have no thoughts.
I'm feeling nothing.
My heart is racing.
Breaths are shallow.
What is sitting on my chest.
Where are my thoughts?
What do I think?
Refresh.
New thoughts.
It's hard to ponder .
Things I'll never say.
Not today.
But someday, I wonder.
I'm going to barf.
A noose from a scarf.
Refresh.
Pop, pop, pop.
Fade slowly into the night.
Everything will be alright.
Walking towards the light.
I'll see you on the other side.
Refresh.
Such a pretty hue.
Complements to cyan.
Watch it swirl.

Round and round.
Strength, I let you go.
Power off.

You won't.

I keep saying I'm okay.
I'm an actor in a play.
The lines, rehearsed.
Look at my smile.
You'd never guess,
My stomach's filled with bile.
Tears making a mess.
You won't make me say.
I'm not okay.

Tin.

I feel my eyelids getting heavy.
Each blink is a little longer.
Each breath is a little deeper.
My mind is still racing.
My heart is still aching.
Internal battles.
Mind versus heart.
I'm made of tin.
Guess who will win

Forevermore.

I want to float away.
It would be so easy.
I would just lay around all day.
Nothing would ever make me queasy.

My mind is wandering.
My thoughts want to be untethered.
Floating away.
Free to drown me.

In the distance I see
Something calling to me.
But I just want to be free
Go away shadowy figure

I can't do this anymore.

Maybe.

Who to trust
Knowing that is a must
The world is not just
Maybe it's all lust
I'd hate to know
My mind now dealt this blow
That'll be going through my head
All night until I'm --

Too little.

Oh how I wish you were here. With you, things are so much clearer. That look in your eye, it carries so much pride. When will we reunite? Let's not dream, keep our heads on straight. And remember why we are here in the first place. No one said this would be easy, but we knew this already. Stay strong and let's move along. Don't worry. I love you.I always have. My feelings for you are not buried. Man, I'm stupid. How could I let you go? I'm stupid for doing so. I still don't understand why you love me. I've done nothing. You say I'm pretty, but am I trustworthy? That's a dumb question. I know you believe otherwise. I'm sorry for all my lies. I wish you'd forgive me, but do I deserve that much sympathy? No? Thought so. It's okay. I don't hate you. I know you
have you more faith in me than I do. I wish things would go back to how they were. Simply much better. 12 weeks left, before I can see you again. I mean, if you want to. I miss hugging you and kissing you. Is that too much to ask for? Let me know before I go. It's bed time, I should sleep. Close your eyes and dream. I promise to do the same.

Ramblings.

Good night to you
I wish I could say
But the words, they just
Seem to fade every
I can't tell you
I love you
Or that I miss you so
I must suffer through this misery
All on my own
You want to be friends
And I'll try really hard
But am I stupid
For even giving you that chance.
You've hurt me deeply
I didn't deserve this.
All I did was love you
And ended up lonely
Why did I trust you
My heart was so foolish
I should've listened to my head.
It knew what it was doing
That day my head made me cry
My heart won the battle
And from that moment on
The war would never be won

Spiraled out of control
I couldn't avoid it
Heartbreak at the end of the road.
I didn't deserve it.
I lay here in bed.
Tortured and angry
Sometimes I wish love
Was only baloney
And then I could say.
I never even cared
I only used you
For some fun affair
But that's not the truth
You and I both know it
I really do love you
And I've always shown it
But you just don't trust me
What am I to do?
I cannot make you see
What I feel for you
I wish I could curse you
Lay spells upon you
But all I wish is that
You find your faith in the darkness.
Black void that's your heart
Find the way out.
Love someone else.
Let me move on.
I'll never forgive myself.

Forgiven.

Through it all
Lies and deceptions
Secrets and schemes
I just wish I could take it all back
And then I wouldn't lack
The ability to say
"I forgive you.
I forgive your betrayal.
I forgive your lies.
I forgive your "I love yous"
I forgive your smiles.
I forgive your hugs.
I forgive your kisses.
I forgive your unnecessary deception."
Because I can't forgive you at all.

Physics.

The light at the end of the tunnel is not always
what it seems. Sometimes you should shy away,,
sometimes you should just proceed. Whichever
way you choose, it makes no difference. It isn't
what you think, you will suffer either way. Shy
away
and you'll always wonder. Know the truth and
you'll be disappointed. Light.
Just a bunch of radiation. Don't be fooled. It's
just a physics trick.